Dear Parent:
Your child's love of reading starts here!

Every child learns to read in a different way and at his or her own speed. Some go back and forth between reading levels and read favorite books again and again. Others read through each level in order. You can help your young reader improve and become more confident by encouraging his or her own interests and abilities. From books your child reads with you to the first books he or she reads alone, there are I Can Read Books for every stage of reading:

SHARED READING
Basic language, word repetition, and whimsical illustrations, ideal for sharing with your emergent reader

BEGINNING READING
Short sentences, familiar words, and simple concepts for children eager to read on their own

READING WITH HELP
Engaging stories, longer sentences, and language play for developing readers

READING ALONE
Complex plots, challenging vocabulary, and high-interest topics for the independent reader

ADVANCED READING
Short paragraphs, chapters, and exciting themes for the perfect bridge to chapter books

I Can Read Books have introduced children to the joy of reading since 1957. Featuring award-winning authors and illustrators and a fabulous cast of beloved characters, I Can Read Books set the standard for beginning readers.

A lifetime of discovery begins with the magical words **"I Can Read!"**

Visit www.icanread.com for information
on enriching your child's reading experience.

Pete the Cat and the Lost Tooth
Copyright © 2017 by James Dean
All rights reserved. Manufactured in the United States of America.
www.icanread.com

Library of Congress Control Number: 2017932863
ISBN 978-0-06-267519-4 (trade bdg.) — ISBN 978-0-06-267518-7 (pbk.)

17 18 19 20 21   LSCC   10 9 8 7 6 5   ❖   First Edition

Pete the Cat
AND THE LOST TOOTH

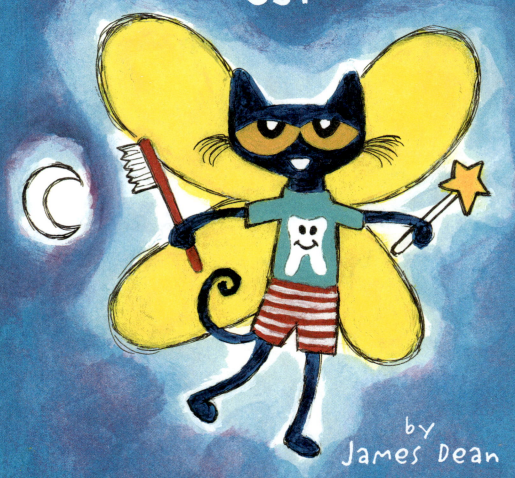

by
James Dean

HARPER
An Imprint of HarperCollinsPublishers

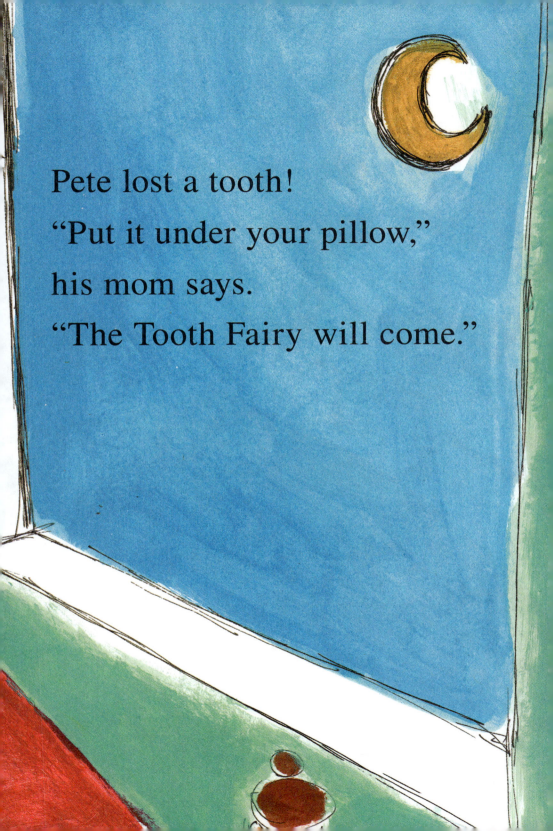

Pete lost a tooth!
"Put it under your pillow,"
his mom says.
"The Tooth Fairy will come."

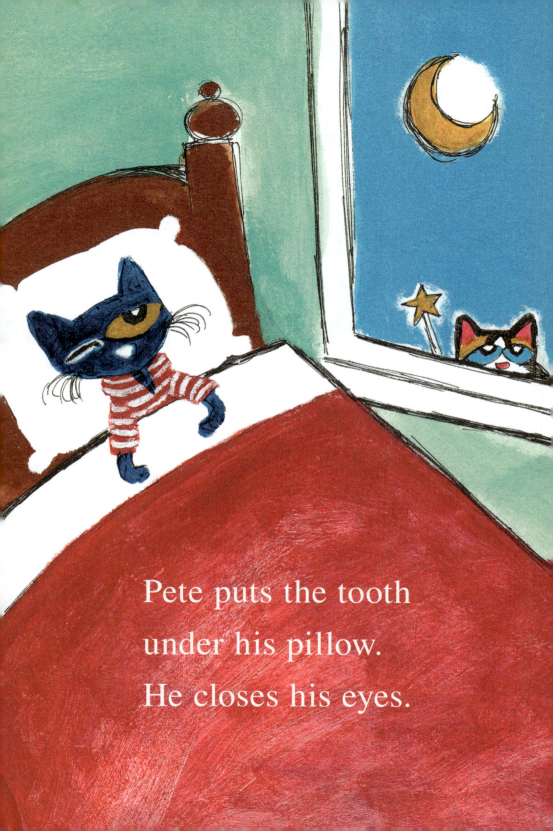

Pete puts the tooth
under his pillow.
He closes his eyes.

He hears a jingle.

It is the Tooth Fairy!

"I am very busy tonight,"
she says.
"I can help!" says Pete.

"Great!"
She gives Pete magic wings.
He can fly!

"Visit these cool kids,"
says the Tooth Fairy.

"Just take the tooth and leave
a coin," she says.
Pete is ready to go!

Callie is first on the list.

There is Callie's lost tooth!

Pete takes the tooth.

He leaves a coin for Callie.

Alligator is next
on the list.

Look!

Alligator's lost tooth!

Careful! It is very sharp.

Pete takes the tooth.

He leaves a coin

for Alligator.

Gus the Platypus is
next on the list.

Uh-oh!

Where is the tooth?

The tooth is not here.

The tooth is not there.

The tooth is not anywhere!

Where is Gus's lost tooth?

The lost tooth is lost!

Does Pete panic?

Nope! He knows what to do.

Look! Gus is awake.

"Where is your tooth, Gus?"

Pete asks.

"Platypuses do not have teeth,"
says Gus.

"But I still want to be a part
of the Tooth Fairy fun!"

"No worries!" says Pete.
Pete puts a coin
under Gus's pillow.

"Thank you!" Gus says.

"You're welcome," says Pete.

"Good night, Gus!"

"Great work, Pete!" says
the Tooth Fairy.

"No problem!" says Pete.

Not everyone is the same.

But being kind is always cool.